Gila Monsters

by Conrad J. Storad

Lerner Publications Company • Minneapolis

To my brothers, Mike, Jim, David, and Joe, and sister Carolyn. You're the best!

Special thanks to Professor Dale DeNardo and Director of Technology Integration and Outreach Charles Kazilek at Arizona State University's School of Life Sciences. The information, access to Gila monsters in the laboratory, and photography you provided were essential to the completion of this book.

The photographs in this book are used with the permission of: © age fotostock/SuperStock, *pp. 4, 8, 22, 25;* © Tim Flach/Stone/Getty Images, *p. 6;* © Andreas Feininger/Time & Life Pictures/Getty Images, *p. 7;* © David W. Middleton/SuperStock, *p. 9;* © Joe & Mary Ann McDonald/Visuals Unlimited, *p. 10;* © C. J. Kazilek, *pp. 11, 13, 15, 23, 24, 28, 38, 40, 48 (bottom);* © Joe McDonald/Visuals Unlimited, *pp. 12, 27, 47;* © Robert J. Erwin/Photo Researchers, Inc., *p. 14;* © David Muench/CORBIS, *p. 16;* © Jack Dykinga/Stone/Getty Images, *p. 17;* © Jonathan Blair/CORBIS, *p. 18;* © John Cancalosi/naturepl.com, *p. 19;* © ZSSD/ SuperStock, *p. 20;* © Curtis Martin/Lonely Planet Images/Getty Images, *p. 21;* © Jim Merli/Visuals Unlimited, *pp. 26, 31, 32, 33, 34;* © David A. Northcott/CORBIS, *p. 29;* © Gerald & Buff Corsi/Visuals Unlimited, *p. 30;* © Walter Meayers Edwards/National Geographic/Getty Images, *p. 35;* © Randy Wells/Stone/Getty Images, *p. 36;* © Patricio Robles Gil/Sierra Madre/Minden Pictures/Getty Images, *p. 37;* © Jeff Foott/Discovery Channel Images/Getty Images, *p. 39;* © Altrendo Nature/Getty Images, *p. 41;* John C. Phillips/Arizona State University Office of Research Publications, *p. 42;* © Rick and Nora Bowers/Visuals Unlimited, *p. 43;* © DEA/L. Romano/De Agostini Picture Library/Getty Images, *p. 46;* © Altrendo Panoramic/Getty Images, *p. 48 (top).*
Cover: © age fotostock/SuperStock.

Lerner Publications Company
A division of Lerner Publishing Group, Inc.
241 First Avenue North
Minneapolis, MN 55401 U.S.A.

Website address: www.lernerbooks.com

Library of Congress Cataloging-in-Publication Data

Storad, Conrad J.
    Gila monsters / by Conrad J. Storad.
       p.   cm. — (Early bird nature books)
    Includes index.
    ISBN 978–0–8225–7888–8 (lib. bdg. : alk. paper)
    1. Gila monster—Juvenile literature. I. Title.
QL666.L247S76 2008
597.95'952—dc22   2007023937

Manufactured in the United States of America
1 2 3 4 5 6 – JR – 13 12 11 10 09 08

Contents

Gila monsters live in the United States and Mexico. The yellow area shows exactly where Gila monsters live.

CANADA

UNITED STATES

MEXICO

N

Be a Word Detective

Can you find these words as you read about the Gila monster's life? Be a detective and try to figure out what they mean. You can turn to the glossary on page 46 for help.

burrows	**glands**	**prey**
camouflage	**hatch**	**reptiles**
desert	**home range**	**scales**
ectotherms	**predators**	**venom**

Chapter 1

This animal is a Gila (HEE-luh) monster. Gila monsters are reptiles. What are some other reptiles?

Meet the Monster

Monsters exist. If you go to the desert, you may see one. But don't be afraid. These monsters are very shy. They are big lizards called Gila monsters.

Lizards belong to a group of animals called reptiles. Snakes are reptiles. So are crocodiles and tortoises. Reptiles' bodies are covered with scales. Scales are flat, hard plates. They protect reptiles' skin.

Desert tortoises are reptiles.

Reptiles are ectotherms. An ectotherm is an animal whose body temperature changes when the outside temperature changes. Ectotherms lie in the sun to warm up. If they get too hot, they go into the shade to cool down.

This Gila monster is resting inside a dead cactus. The cactus protects the lizard from the hot sun.

The Gila monster is the biggest lizard in all of North America. An adult Gila monster is up to 2 feet long. That's as long as two rulers laid end to end. It weighs up to 5 pounds. That's what a small bag of flour weighs.

The scientific name of the Gila monster is Heloderma suspectum.

Gila monsters have long, sharp claws.

The big lizard has a thick body and a
short, fat tail. It has four stubby legs. Each foot
has five long toes. The toes are tipped with
sharp claws.

A Gila monster's tongue is forked. The tip of the tongue has two points.

The Gila monster has a large head. Its eyes are small and dark. In its mouth are many sharp, curved teeth. The lizard has a long, black, forked tongue.

A Gila monster's skin is covered with round scales.

Gila monsters are beautiful animals. They are covered with short, round scales. The scales look like tiny beads. They are black, orange, pink, or yellow. The scales form patches and stripes on the lizard's skin.

No two Gila monsters look exactly alike.
But the lizards come in two main color patterns.
Gila monsters are either banded or reticulated
(ruh-TIHK-yoo-lay-tihd).

This is a reticulated Gila monster. Its body has patches of colored scales.

*This is a banded Gila monster. Its body has
wide stripes with spots inside them.*

Banded Gila monsters have wide black
stripes on their bodies and tails. Between the
stripes are light-colored scales. These lizards
look like black-striped candy canes.

Reticulated Gila monsters have black stripes
on their tails. But they don't have stripes on
their bodies. Their bodies have patches of light
and dark scales.

The scale patterns are camouflage (KAM-uh-flahzh). They help Gila monsters hide. The lizards rest in places with patches of sun and shade. It is hard to see a Gila monster in these places. The lizard's light and dark patches blend in with light and dark spots on the ground.

This Gila monster's scales are the same colors as the sandy desert soil.

Chapter 2

The Gila monster was named after the Gila River. This river runs through deserts where Gila monsters live. What are deserts?

Life Underground

Gila monsters live in the southwestern United States and northwestern Mexico. They

16

live in deserts. Deserts are places that do not get much rain. The Gila monster's home gets very hot in the summer. In the winter, the desert is cooler.

Most banded Gila monsters live in the Mojave (muh-HAH-vee) Desert. This desert is in southeastern California and parts of Nevada, Arizona, and Utah.

Four young burrowing owls are standing at the entrance to their burrow.

Many desert animals live in holes in the ground. These holes are called burrows. On hot summer days, the burrows are much cooler than the outside air. On chilly winter days, the burrows are warmer than the outside air.

Gila monsters spend most of their lives underground. Some Gila monsters live in cracks under big piles of rocks. Others stay in burrows that other animals dug.

Each Gila monster looks for the perfect burrow. Some holes are too small. There isn't enough room for the lizard to turn around. Some burrows aren't deep enough. They don't stay cool enough on hot days. When a Gila monster finds just the right burrow, it lives there year after year.

Gila monsters spend most of their time alone. But sometimes two or more Gila monsters share a burrow.

On hot days, the Gila monster stays cool in its burrow. If the lizard gets chilly, it comes out of its burrow. It warms its body in the sun.

In the winter, it is too cold for Gila monsters to go outside. They stay in their burrows all winter long. They come out when the desert warms up in the spring.

This Gila monster is warming up in a sunny place.

The southwestern desert is cool in the winter. Sometimes snow covers the ground.

A Gila monster never travels more than 1 mile from its burrow. The area the lizard lives in is called its home range. The home range is the Gila monster's neighborhood. It is where the lizard looks for food.

Chapter 3

Gila monsters hunt and eat other animals. How does a Gila monster's tongue help it find animals?

Lizard Feasts

Gila monsters are predators (PREH-duh-turz). Predators are animals that hunt and eat other animals. The animals a Gila monster hunts are called its prey (PRAY).

A Gila monster licks the air to find prey. When you lick an ice cream cone, chemicals (KEH-muh-kuhlz) stick to your tongue. Those chemicals help you taste the ice cream. When a Gila monster licks the air, chemicals from the air stick to its tongue. The big lizard can smell chemicals that are on its tongue. The chemicals tell the Gila monster when other animals are nearby.

This Gila monster is using its tongue to find food.

Gila monsters bite their prey to kill it. The lizards have venom (VEH-nuhm). Venom is a poison. Gila monsters use their venom to kill prey. Rattlesnakes use venom the same way.

A Gila monster's venom comes from its venom glands. A gland is a part of the body that makes a liquid. Glands in your mouth make saliva (suh-LYE-vuh). The glands in a Gila monster's mouth make venom.

A Gila monster's venom glands are in the bottom of its mouth.

A Gila monster is eating a mouse.

When a Gila monster finds prey, it bites the prey hard. The lizard usually doesn't let go right away. It may chew on its prey for more than 15 minutes. As the Gila monster chews, venom slowly soaks into the prey. The venom kills the prey.

This Gila monster has found some bird eggs.

Gila monsters can't run fast. They look for prey that is easy to catch. Gila monsters eat small animals such as baby birds, mice, and rats.

Eggs are the Gila monster's favorite food. The lizard doesn't have to run fast to catch an egg. It just has to find a nest with eggs in it. Gila monsters eat birds' eggs. They also eat the eggs of tortoises, snakes, and lizards. Sometimes a Gila monster swallows a whole egg. But usually it breaks the egg open. Then it licks out the gooey insides.

Gila monsters don't need to eat often. They may eat only a few meals each year. Gila monsters do most of their hunting during the spring and early summer. They can find lots of food then. Many animals lay eggs in the spring. Many baby animals are born then too.

When a Gila monster finds food, it eats as much as it can. This Gila monster is eating eggs.

Most of a Gila monster's fat is stored inside its tail. If the lizard goes a long time without eating, its tail gets thinner.

Gila monsters can eat a lot of food at a time. An adult Gila monster can eat one-third of its weight at one meal. That's like a 60-pound third grader eating 80 hamburgers!

When the lizard eats, its body changes the food into fat. The fat stays inside the Gila monster's body. Between meals, the lizard's body gets energy from the fat.

Gila monsters can store water in their bodies too. In the summer, thunderstorms bring rain to the desert. The big lizards drink lots of rainwater during these storms. They will need the water when the desert is dry again.

A Gila monster is drinking water.

Chapter 4

Gila monsters hatch from eggs. How big are Gila monsters' eggs?

Little Monsters

Female Gila monsters lay eggs in July or August. Each female uses her claws to dig a shallow hole in the ground. She lays 3 to 12 eggs in the hole. Then the mother Gila monster leaves. She will not come back to take care of her babies.

Gila monster eggs are white and shiny. Each egg is 2 to 3 inches long. That's about as long as a chicken's egg. The eggshell is soft and kind of squishy.

This female Gila monster has laid five eggs.

Babies hatch out of the eggs about 10 months later. They usually hatch in late spring. That is a good time to hatch. There is lots of food for the baby lizards to eat.

A baby Gila monster is hatching out of an egg.

Newly hatched Gila monsters are only a few inches long. But they have a full set of sharp teeth. The babies also have venom. Their scales are brightly colored.

Baby Gila monsters are on their own from the time they hatch. The young lizards can take care of themselves.

A Gila monster's scale pattern may change as it grows.

Baby Gila monsters are always hungry. They hunt for insects, spiders, and worms. They eat and eat and eat. A baby Gila monster can eat half of its own weight each day. That is a lot of food!

Young Gila monsters grow fast. They are fully grown in only three years. Then they are ready to start their own families.

Gila monsters can live up to 25 years.

Chapter 5

In the 1800s, lots of people moved to the southwestern desert. How high did some of these people say Gila monsters could jump?

Danger in the Desert

 Many years ago, lots of people moved to the deserts where Gila monsters live. The people didn't know much about desert animals. They made up many stories about Gila

monsters. One story said a Gila monster's breath could kill small animals or even people. Another story said if a Gila monster bit a person, it would not let go until the sun went down that night. Other people said Gila monsters could jump 2 feet high. None of these stories are true.

Gila monsters can't jump. They can only crawl on the ground.

Gila monsters usually don't hurt people. The big lizards move very slowly. They bite people only to protect themselves. If you leave Gila monsters alone, they will leave you alone.

If a person gets too close to a Gila monster, the lizard will open its mouth and hiss. If the person doesn't leave, the Gila monster may bite.

Coyotes (kye-OH-teez) are related to dogs and wolves. Coyotes eat Gila monsters.

Adult Gila monsters are big. But they are food for other desert predators. Coyotes eat adult Gila monsters. So do large owls, hawks, and eagles. Snakes and large lizards eat baby Gila monsters. And lots of animals eat Gila monster eggs.

Sometimes Gila monsters crawl onto roads or parking lots. Some of these Gila monsters get run over by cars.

Humans are the biggest danger to Gila monsters. Many people have moved to the places where Gila monsters live. When the big lizards try to cross roads, they may get squashed by cars and trucks.

Most people will never see a wild Gila monster. If you do see one, you are lucky. But remember that Gila monsters are not pets.

They are wild animals. They have sharp teeth and dangerous venom.

In the state of Arizona, Gila monsters are protected. People are not allowed to keep the lizards as pets. And it is against the law to kill a Gila monster.

Gila monsters live in the Sonoran Desert. This desert covers most of southwestern Arizona.

*This scientist studies Gila monsters. He holds
the lizards carefully so they cannot bite him.*

Scientists study Gila monsters. They want to learn more about the big lizards. Scientists in Arizona are studying how far Gila monsters travel. To do this, they put tiny radios inside Gila monsters' bodies. The radios do not hurt the animals. The scientists use the radios to track the Gila monsters. They are learning lots of new things about these interesting lizards.

The Gila monster knows how to live in the desert. It has been there for thousands of years. We need to protect the big lizard so it will continue to survive. The world wouldn't be the same without Gila monsters.

Gila monsters are an important part of the southwestern desert.

ON SHARING A BOOK

When you share a book with a child, you show that reading is important. To get the most out of the experience, read in a comfortable, quiet place. Turn off the television and limit other distractions, such as telephone calls.

Be prepared to start slowly. Take turns reading parts of this book. Stop occasionally and discuss what you're reading. Talk about the photographs. If the child begins to lose interest, stop reading. When you pick up the book again, revisit the parts you have already read.

BE A VOCABULARY DETECTIVE

The word list on page 5 contains words that are important in understanding the topic of this book. Be word detectives and search for the words as you read the book together. Talk about what the words mean and how they are used in the sentence. Do any of these words have more than one meaning? You will find the words defined in a glossary on page 46.

WHAT ABOUT QUESTIONS?

Use questions to make sure the child understands the information in this book. Here are some suggestions:

> What did this paragraph tell us? What does this picture show? Besides lizards, what are some other kinds of reptiles? Where do Gila monsters live? How often do Gila monsters eat? How long does it take a baby Gila monster to grow up? What is your favorite part of the book? Why?

If the child has questions, don't hesitate to respond with questions of your own, such as What do *you* think? Why? What is it that you don't know? If the child can't remember certain facts, turn to the index.

INTRODUCING THE INDEX

The index helps readers find information without searching through the whole book. Turn to the index on page 48. Choose an entry such as *food* and ask the child to use the index to find out what Gila monsters eat. Repeat with as many entries as you like. Ask the child to point out the differences between an index and a glossary. (The index helps readers find information, while the glossary tells readers what words mean.)

LEARN MORE ABOUT
GILA MONSTERS

BOOKS

Dunphy, Madeleine. *Here Is the Southwestern Desert*. Berkeley, CA: Web of Life Children's Books, 2006. Learn about the Sonoran Desert, one of the deserts in which Gila monsters live.

Johnson, Rebecca L. *A Walk in the Desert*. Minneapolis: Lerner Publications Company, 2001. Find out about other plants and animals that live in North American deserts.

Miller, Jake. *The Gila Monster*. New York: PowerKids Press, 2003. Find out more about the largest lizard in the United States.

Souza, D. M. *Packed with Poison!: Deadly Animal Defenses*. Minneapolis: Millbrook Press, 2006. This book has information on many different animals that use poison to catch food or protect themselves.

Wilson, Hannah. *Life-Size Reptiles*. New York: Sterling Children's Books, 2007. This book has amazing photos of lizards, snakes, tortoises, and other reptiles.

WEBSITES

DesertUSA
http://www.desertusa.com/life.html
This Web page has information on North America's deserts and the plants and animals that live in them.

Reptiles
http://www.stlzoo.org/animals/abouttheanimals/reptiles
Find out about the different kinds of reptiles—alligators and crocodiles, lizards, snakes, turtles and tortoises, and tuataras.

Reptiles: Lizard
http://www.sandiegozoo.org/animalbytes/t-lizard.html
Learn more about lizards through this website, which includes video, sound, and photos.

GLOSSARY

burrows: holes in the ground that animals live in

camouflage (KAM-uh-flahzh): color patterns that help animals hide

desert: a place where little rain falls

ectotherms: animals whose body temperature changes when the outside temperature changes. Some people call ectotherms cold-blooded animals.

glands: parts of the body that make liquids. Glands in a Gila monster's mouth make venom.

hatch: to come out of an egg

home range: the area a Gila monster lives in

predators (PREH-duh-turz): animals that hunt and eat other animals

prey (PRAY): animals that are hunted and eaten by other animals

reptiles: animals whose bodies are covered with scales. Lizards, snakes, crocodiles, and tortoises are reptiles.

scales: flat, hard plates that protect a Gila monster's skin

venom (VEH-nuhm): poison. Gila monsters use venom to kill their prey.

INDEX

Pages listed in **bold** type refer to photographs.